Walter Garstang

My Heart's Fruit-Garden

Walter Garstang

My Heart's Fruit-Garden

ISBN/EAN: 9783744734578

Printed in Europe, USA, Canada, Australia, Japan

Cover: Foto ©Thomas Meinert / pixelio.de

More available books at **www.hansebooks.com**

My Heart's Fruit-Garden

Wherein are Divers Delectable Adages and Similes
of the Prince of Doctrinal Ethics:

A TRANSLATION, OUT OF THE ANCIENT BIBLICAL HEBREW, OF

THE BOOK OF KOHÉLETH

ELSE

"ECCLESIASTES, OR THE PREACHER."

BY

WALTER GARSTANG, M.D.,

Collegiate of the Royal College of Physicians, in London and in Edinburgh;
Fellow of the Royal College of Surgeons in Edinburgh;
Author of Kindred Versions of the Scriptural Poems,
Joel, and " The Sacred Eclogue (Song of Songs)."

Λάβε τὸ βιβλαρίδιον καὶ κατάφαγε αὐτό·
καὶ πικρανεῖ σου τὴν κοιλίαν, ἀλλ' ἐν τῷ στόματί
σου ἔσται γλυκὺ ὡς μέλι.—ΑΠΟΚ. Κεφ. x. 9.

LONDON: SIMPKIN, MARSHALL & CO.
LIVERPOOL: EDWARD HOWELL.

1886

𝔚ords 𝔇edicatory.

TO HER

WHO IS LANGUISHING

IS AFFECTIONATELY INSCRIBED

" My Heart's Fruit-Garden,"

IN SURE AND CERTAIN HOPE

THAT

HEREAFTER

AT THE GREAT DAY

SHE SHALL BE FOUND AWAKENED

OUT OF THE DUST UNTO

EVERLASTING

LIFE.

W. G.

Blackburn, *September*, 1886.

SOME PRECEPTIVE SAYINGS

Kohéleth Son of David,

COUNSELLOR IN JERUSALEM.

Page 49, line 10—*for* is *read* in.

an man :

by the whole of his operose production,
at which he will take pains beneath the solar Light.

4 A descending Cycle of creatures departeth,
at the same time an ascending Cycle cometh ;
thus into unlimited time the World is holding on.

5 For the solar Light broke forth,
and that solar Light went in ;
still in its place—
vehemently swallowing up air at the focus !—
the same is rising, there.

SOME PRECEPTIVE SAYINGS

OF

Kohéleth Son of David,

COUNSELLOR IN JERUSALEM.

2   Most vain! most instable, said Kohéleth,
a whiff—quickliest passing and gone;—
the whole is instable, counterfeit entity!

3   What gainfulness? is there to the plebeian man:
by the whole of his operose production,
at which he will take pains beneath the solar Light.

4 A descending Cycle of creatures departeth,
at the same time an ascending Cycle cometh;
thus into unlimited time the World is holding on.

5 For the solar Light broke forth,
and that solar Light went in;
still in its place—
vehemently swallowing up air at the focus!—
the same is rising, there.

6   Moving forward towards the South;
then turning round, towards the North :
wending round about, encompassing ;—
is bearing forward the Wind;
so over its circuits ordinarily turned the Wind.

7   All of the Brooks flow unto the Sea;
though as for the Sea, there is no more existence of
     it full :
at the place, in which the Brooks are disappearing,
there ! they are about to come back, in order to
     flowing.

8   The entierty of things actively at work,
a gifted man shall not be able to properly speak :
eye shall not satisfy, to viewing;
and ear shall not surfeit, from hearing.

9   What thing soever was,
is the selfsame which shall be ;
and as for whatever action was done,
that same is which shall be done :
as there is no new thing extant, below the solar
     Light.

10   Is there a case ?
about which it may hap one sayeth,
" behold now ! that is new": erst,

the same had existed at no great distance from
    hidden ages,

time which was away from our faces.

11 Remembrance is not extant, respecting our fore-
    fathers :

so also as respects the later races who shall be,

there shall respecting them be by no means remem-
    brance ;

equally with the races who will come after.

12   I am devoted to Kohéleth ;

I have been an adviser! under Israel, in Jerusalem.

13 So I placed at my heart to inquire

and to eagerly search, according to a certain
    science ;—

concerning whatsoever had been transacted,

under the solar Light :

that—an employ of badness—a god hath rendered

to the sons of the mere man, that they may ply
    in it.

14 I have looked at the whole of the doings

which have been wrought under the solar Light :

behold even as to the whole !

it is fruitless breath, namely a companioness of
    wind.

15   A thing made crooked,
> will not be a potent one for becoming straight:
> and defectiveness will not so be made capable
> as to be appointed.

16   I, my very self in the presence of my heart, did
>   confidently speak,
> so as to say—"as for me! behold `
> " I have aggrandised and enlarged with wisdom,
> " above the measure of every one
> " who hath been before me over Jerusalem:
> " and as for my heart,
> " it hath enjoyed in great degree science and
>   learning:

17   " I may now (please God) give my heart to know-
>   ing experience ;
> " and that, to knowing vain-gloriousness, which is
>   folly":
> I have come to know, that the same likewise,
> is a fellowship of wind.

18   Of a truth ! co-existent with greatness of experience,
> there is abundance of vexation:
> so he who actually addeth to knowledge,
> doth in effect enlarge a source of pain.

CHAPTER II.

1   I admonished me, in the manner of my heart—
" come thou directly, I pray!
" I will thence essay thee in gladness,
" so view thou in pleasantness":
but lo also that, is a profitless breath.

2   At laughter, I railed "Oh he's one seized with
      madness!"
and at merriment, "Oh how the soft thing is
   acting!"

3   I espied within my heart for that action,
whereby is a pulling along at my flesh by the
      wine:
my heart moreover a movent, which driveth dex-
      terously,—
in this way to a holding fast in foolishness,
up to the time, at which I might observe,
where the moral good beareth to the sons of the
      plebeian man,
which they must practise under these heavens;
the number, all told, of the days of their life.

4 I made great, with regard to my undertakings:
I set up to my own use buildings;
I planted in supply of myself vineyards.

5 I made in adaptation of myself;—
gardens, and especially paradises:
as I stuck in within them,
trees of every sort of fruit.

6 I made for myself channels of water:
on purpose to irrigate out of them;—
a thicket, consisting of shooting-up trees.

7 I purchased male-servants and female slaves;
and as for begotten-ones of the palace,
the several became mine own:
even a purchase—oxen and sheep far amounting—
        became mine,
more than all, which were at my face in Jerusalem.

8 I brought together with appropriation to me,
also silver and gold,
as well the precious privy possession of Kings,
as of the jurisdictional circles:
I appointed on the part of myself,
male and female vocalists!
and, sooth to say! some sensuous delights
befitting the sons of the earthly man,—
ladies a very many.

9 So I grew and increased in comparison of each
who had been at my face in Jerusalem:
my experience, it is added, did minister to me.

10 Because whatsoever mine eyes demanded,
I put not aside from them:

I bridled not at my heart,
from the smallest part of every kind of gladness!
since my heart rejoiced for the merit of all my labour;
and such as this was my portion because of all my
labour.

11 But I personally turned the face,
unto all my doings, which my hands had wrought;
and unto my laboursome effect,
which I had taken pains for accomplishing:
when behold the whole is ostentation,
and that a nice consociate of wind;
as gainfulness is not extant under the solar Light.

12 Hereupon I turned me the face to regard experience,
to wit, fooleries and foolishness:
nay but what quality is the mere man? who shall
come in
after the King, he in particular whom long ago
they anointed.

13　Nay I saw personally that to the expertness,
　　in comparison of inexpertness,
　　there is existing a gainfulness:
　　somewhat like the gainfulness of light,
　　in comparison of the darkness.

14　As for the dexterous man, his eyes are with his
　　　　head;
　　and as for the sinistrous fellow, he in the darkness
　　　　proceedeth:
　　although I have come to know, yea I myself,
　　that singular hap-hazard—one and the same,
　　is accustomed to meet against the whole of them.

15　At the same time I bespoke me in my heart,—
　　" well-nigh a particular hap-hazard of the unwary
　　　　mortal
　　" shall befall me likewise; so then for what purpose?
　　" at that time overmuch did I get myself insight":
　　but I well spoke, that even here is vain-glorious
　　　　breath.

16　　There is verily no existence of remembrance to the
　　well-advised man! not without the indocile fellow,
　　　　for ever:
　　in that already, at these days which come in,
　　the whole was fallen into oblivion;

lo how ! the well-versed man shall die,
in like manner as the unversed mortal.

17   Whereupon I loathed at life itself;
for detrimental against me is that performing,
which hath been transacted, under the solar Light:
indeed the whole is a profitless vapour,
and that a companioness of wind.

18   I particularly then loathed at my whole effect of
    labour,
    where I am an industrious person, under the beamy
      Sun:
    considering that I must leave it for the mere man,
    who shall be at the rear of myself.

19   And yet what person foreseeth,
    whether he shall be the witted man,
    or I lief say a witless fellow ?
    still he will have sovereignty in all my effect of
      toil,
    as to which I took pains and which I excogitated,
    under the solar Light:
    here also is a repining breath.

20   Therefore I surrounded me,
    on purpose to cast off all hopes at my heart:

for sake, even of the whole of the effect of toil,
which I endeavoured earnestly under the solar Light.

21 Observe there is a human being in existence,
the production of whose pains! is in
supernal science, and in rudiment, and in œconomics:
howbeit to a man, with whom not is industry upon
　　it,
he shall give it after the manner of his share;
this really is transitory breath, and a great mishap.

22 But indeed what is it which ariseth for the mere
　　man?
by all his excessive pains,
and especially by cogitation, acted in his heart:
seeing that he is a hard-working man,
beneath the resplendent Sun.

23 Is it not! that all his days are incitation of pain?
and that chagrin is his distracting employ?
likewise in the night, his heart by no means hath
　　rested:
this indeed! is unprofitableness itself.

24 There is no existence of beneficial influence in the
　　mere man,
that he will eat and will have drunk,
so that he hath caused at his soul
to see luckiness in the result of his toil:

really this I personally have experienced,
that surely from the hand of the Deity it cometh
    down.
25 Because what person will eat ? or who make haste,
out into public view rather than I myself ?
26 I avouch that with relation to the earthly man,
to him who is virtuous at His face,
He   hath   deigned   science, and conception, and
    rejoicing :
while yet upon the sinning-man He hath laid out
a course of life to scraping together and to collecting !
in order that he may contribute to one virtuous
in the sight of the Deity ;
much is this a luckless breath,
namely a compeeress of common air.

CHAPTER III.

1   For the whole, there is determinate time:
and specially time for every purpose below these
heavens.

2   Time becometh for bearing, and time for dying:
time for planting, and time for rooting up one
planted.

3   Time for sticking, and time for healing;
time for breaking through, and time for building up.

4   Time for weeping, also time for laughing;
time to be piercing with woe,
and time for leaping with joy.

5   Time serveth for casting forth stones;
and there ariseth a time of the bringing of stones
together:
time for embracing;
and time, even for going far away from eagerly
clasping.

6   Time for earnestly seeking, and time for pronouncing
lost;
time for keeping, and time for flinging away.

7 Time for tearing asunder,
and time for sewing together;
time for being silent, and time for speaking.

8 Time for loving, and time for hating;
time serving for battle, and time tending to peace.

9 Is anything of advantage? concerning the worker,
in respect of what he is an industrious man.

10 I have occupied at the carking calling!
which gods have each condescended to appoint
to the sons of the earthly man, in order to ply in it.

11 Touching the whole that He hath made,
it is handsome in its own time:
likewise this finite durableness
He hath inserted in their heart;
so that it not at all obtains! that the mere man
shall arrive at the creation, such!
as the Deity has put into action,
from commencement and stretching forth up to
    completion.

12 I have come to know, accordingly,
there is non-existence of the good in them:
sure then it is whene'er one hath been cheerful,
and hath done the right throughout his life.

13 Even then anyone of the humankind,
    who shall so eat, that he have drunk,
    and have seen fortune's goods as an effect of his toil:
    a gift of gods the same is.

14 I have closely observed a matter—the great fact!
    that whate'er the Godhead hath done and still con-
            tinueth so to do,
    this selfsame thing shall exist up to eternity;
    over and above it, there existeth not that may be
            adjoined;
    and off it, there existeth not the least portion for
            retrenching:
    the Godhead thus hath dealt,
    that creatures may fear from the presence of Him-
            self.

15 Anything which had been, the same is already;
    and anything that is going to take place,
    hath long ago come to pass:
    yet for the part of Deity Himself,
    He is e'er vigilantly seeking out the affair pursued
            now!

16   Yet still I saw that which is beneath the splendent
            Sun:

a place of judgment, there where is the injustice;
and especially a place of acquittal, there where is
    the guiltiness.

17 I charged me in my heart—
" upon the just one, as against the party guilty,
" let the Godhead pronounce sentence :
" when there is time for every sort of way of pro-
    ceeding;
" so for the merit of the whole of the conduct,
    then."

18 I charged me in my heart,
after a deliverance, in vogue among the sons of
    mere men,
" O for severing them ! may the Godhead be :
" thus alway to see, that they are bears themselves
    to themselves ! "

19 Is it not ! that an odd occurrence are the descend-
    ants of Adam,
and that an odd occurrence are the dumb beasts;
even one and the same accident is current to them;
how an exanimate state is of the one,
so kindred as possible is the exanimate state of the
    other;
whilst a sole vivifying aëriform element,
extendeth unto the whole:

therefore the notional quantum of the human being
apart from the dumb beast, is nothing;
indeed the whole is nothingness.

20 The whole is going towards one and the same place:
the whole hath come into being from off the mould;
and the whole is going back, into its pristine
earthy state.

2! Is anybody having cognisance?
as to the ghost of the descendants of mere man,
the same which mounteth aloft:
or touching the ghost of the reasonless beast,
the same which sinketh adown, even into the land.

22 Thus I saw! that there is no existence of a goodly
condition,
apart from when the plebeian man
is accustomably joyful with his own performings;
for of course that particular, is his own share:
because whoever can bring him in?
that he may look with gladness on anything
which shall arise late at the back of himself.

CHAPTER IV.

1   I thereupon turned back
into that state of self, whence I had set out;
in that I would look at mostwhat all the extortions :
as those being perpetrated beneath the splendent
     Sun :
behold welaway ! the tears of poor creatures over-
     whelmed !
as there is not present to them a man consoling ;
whilst from the hand of their extorters, there is
     force.

2 Wherefore in amity am I ! with one
who strongly panegyriseth the dead, which long
     ago died :
rather than the living ones who—
surviving the violence of their oppressors !—
are the same creatures living, as far as unto this
     pinch.

3 Lucky though, in comparison of both of them,
is conspicuously he who yet was unborn :

forasmuch as he will not have been the subject,

even of this selfsame atrocious deed,

which hath been done beneath the resplendent Sun.

4 But I have in person viewed, as to every kind of toil,

and particularly so, all the lucrative yield of the work ;

how flagrantly ! the same is

an eminent man's objective grudgings, from his neighbour :

yet this is an envious breath,

and indeed a worthless complice of wind.

5 It is the addle-pated wight, folding together with his hands ;

nay biting, at his own flesh.

6 " Delicious," quoth one, " is fulness of a single palm in quietness :

" in comparison to fulness of the two coherent fists !

" under hardship and feeding on bluster."

7 So personally I turned back, that I might view, beneath the luminous Sun, a barren spectacle.

8　Extant is one yet not a second,

also son and brother there exists none to him!

whilst there is not an end to the whole of his
　　labouring ;

even also his eyes, riches will not satiate :

"now for anybody? am I an industrious man,

"and that a man? causing at my life's centre

"to want of a particle of enjoyment";

fruitless breath ! this is really ;—

also a course of life ill-favoured, that is !

9　　Very much more commodious are

the two of the same sort than the one :

for as much there inheres with respect to themselves,

a profitable hire in their wearisome labour.

10　Doubtless if they shall sink down,

the one will raise up the body of his associate :

then woe to him, who is a single one ! if that he
　　sink down,

and there is not a second present to do that action,

whereby he could be reänimated.

11　Quite so, it is clear should two mates lie down,

that it would for them be warm :

whereas with respect to the one alone,
how so? would he become warm.

12 And in case other would overbear him,—the one;
the two mates could stand up against him:
thus the cord, which is threefold spun,
might not in a full-hasty assault, be broken off.

13 Choice comparatively! is a stripling, striving, but
    clear-sighted:
towards a King grey in years, who is wrong-
    headed;
since in self-confident plight!
he hath felt not that he should alway take heed,
    as yet.

14 Lo from the House of prisoners,
there did one march out in order to rule:
albeit the fact likewise that in his kingdom,
he was begotten insignificant.

15 I looked at the collective mass of the living,
these who are going about constantly, under the
    solar Light:
in their midst, I saw this second stripling,
who shall stand instead of him.

16 There is not any close affecting all the people,
    with regard to every sort that had been anterior
        of them;
    to be sure the hinder ones will not be glad over it:
    I aver that this is fruitless breath again,
    and specially meditation of wind.

CHAPTER V.

1   Perform thou punctiliously thy footstep,

in so far as thou wilt go unto the House of the
    Deity,

and thou oughtest to be one nigh at hand rather
    for hearkening,

than for setting the jesters a sacrifice:

although that not any of them is cognizant,

whenever he did an act of wickedness.

2 Do not terrify, over thy mouth,

and especially thy heart do not hurry,—

to causing a matter to go out in the face of the
    Godhead:

that the Godhead abideth in the heavens,

and that thou art upon the earth;

upon an ideal of such sort!

thy sayings shall be numerally few.

3 Mark that the dream came in,

with the bringing together of concernment;

also a fool's voice! with the heaping together of
    words.

4 Just as thou wilt vow a vow to godlike beings!
do not make the least delay, as to the repaying of
  it;
it is that no not willingness! is with the impious:
exactly what thou shalt vow, repay thou.

5 There is ease! when thou wilt not vow:
but not when thou shalt vow, but wilt not perform.

6 Do not give out at thy mouth, so as virtually
to cause thy carnal lusts and passions to sin;
and do not bear forth in the face of the Jehovistic
  messenger—
"lo an hallucination! the thing is":
to what purpose? shall the Godhead storm,
suitably to thy voice,
in order that he shall have caused corruption,
at the occupation of thy hands.

7 It is quite clear in an increasing of phantasms,
and in an increasing of vapours,
that there are words which are greatly erratical:
therefore the Godhead fear thou!

8 There is a probability of violence done to the
  poor,
so if robbery at a seat of justice and power,

thou shalt see within the jurisdiction,

do not be wonderstruck, over that turn:

for a powerful one, away from a powerful one
keepeth watch;

and powerful ones are over them.

9 So then as for a country's benefit,

it is in respect of the whole:

a King serveth for territory being cultivated.

10 Him loving silver, silver shall not satiate;

and anyone loving in stores, what cometh in shall
not:

also this is transitoriness.

11 When that which is riches had multiplied,

they brought together who are devouring it:

well what expediency? tendeth to the possessors of it,

though it be positively an enjoying of his eyes.

12 In sweetness is the sleep of him doing heavy
service,

or if a small or in accomplishing a large quantity
he will eat:

but as to the satiety, belonging to the rich man,
there is   .

inexistence of its causing him to be quiet that he
may sleep.

13   There subsisteth a heartfelt affliction,
which I have seen beneath the resplendent Sun :
an opulent possession! preserved for its lord's use,
against his own unfortunateness.

14 And this self-same possession hath been lost
in a detrimental concernment :
while yet there is the propagating of a child,
though existent in his hand is not any—the least
    thing.

15 Even that which he was come forth from his
    mother's belly,
he—a naked one!—shall turn back so as to go
according to that which he had arrived :
for he shall not carry away by his toil any thing
    at all,
which he might cause to go with his hand.

16   Thus besides, there subsisteth a heartfelt affliction;—
the entire conjuncture how a mortal had arrived,
in this condition he shall move forward :
in what way therefore tendeth behoof to him,
who will yield his strength unto the wind ?

17 Much all his days he in the darkness will tyran-
    nize over :

even of vexation there is no little production ;
and that, too, his sickness continueth and his wrath !

18   Behold, how from personal experience I have known!
how salutary—how beneficial to eat and to drink,
and to perceive prosperity in the whole of his toil,
where a man will spend his strength under the
     beamy Sun,
that number of the days of his life
which the Deity hath assigned him, as that is his
     lot.

19   Even so any one of common men,
on whom the Deity hath bestowed riches and goods,
and hath allowed him to rule to tasting a small
     part thereof,
and indeed to take away materially his share ;
then to be joyous at his act of labouring :
such as this ! a gift of gods, it is.

20   Therefore, not progressively he will think, as to
     the days of his life :
for the Deity is answering in the gladness of his
     heart.

CHAPTER VI.

1   There is existent evil, that I have seen under the beamy Sun:

and vastly the same is come to pass against the humankind.

2 A case, is a notable on whom the Deity shall have conferred riches

both goods and gloriousness, so that existeth not it

lacking at his soul—out of every kind that he will have longed,

yet the Deity will not condescend to let him have power

for rule, to consuming from a small part of it;

as a consequence goodlack! a personage a stranger will devour it:

this is a covetous breath, a penetrative calamity also it is.

3 Though, again, a notable may have begotten a hundred,

and years extended have lived,—

if enough shall have been those,

which are the days of his years! or

else if his soul will not have satiated

from a great deal of that bountifulness;

and a grave withal, had by no means been his:

I had pronounced,—lucky in comparison of him,
   was the abortion.

Since in the bubble it entered,

and so into the darkness it must go away:

thus then it is that with the darkness its being
   will be covered.

5 Alike solary munificence it had not enjoyed, nor
   perceived:

quietude attended this human thing, but not the
   other mortal.

6 But were it granted that so long! another had
   lived

as a thousand of years two times,

and yet had not seen fortune's goods:

good-now! is not the whole moving forward even
   to one place?

7 All toil of the plebeian man concerneth his mouth:

and even then the appetency will not be fulfilled.

8 But yet, what additament belongeth to the versed man

in comparison to the unversed fellow?

what to a son of oppression who hath experience

to the pursuing of a way of life in front of the enjoyers of life?

9 Agreeable by far is the eyes' view, than the soul's hankering:

even also this is boastful breath,

and that a concomitant of wind.

10 With reference to whatever creature hath existed,

the essential thereof hath already been proclaimed :

so one known is that, who is earthy man:

as he shall no more be made capable to contending

against one that is passing strong,

in comparison with himself.

11 Whereas there are affairs in existence which

in acting not a little do propagate boastful breath :

what additament is there, that belongeth to the mere man?

12 Is positively anyone knowing by experience in what way

there is comfortableness for mere man among the lusty ones,

the allotted number! of the days of the life of his
brawling breath,

that he is e'er enacting them in pursuance of the
shadow?

because that, can anybody announce to the mere man,

what must come to pass at his rear, under the
solar Light?

CHAPTER VII.

1   Pleasant is name! beyond redolent oil!
and that too the day of the state of lying dead,
in comparison of the day when one was born.

2 It is good to go to a house of mourning,
rather than to a house of drink;
in as much as that is
the determination of the whole of human-kind:
wherefore the living person will give the same his
    heart.

3 Suitable is grief, more than wantonness:
for by distressfulness of face, a heart will be cheer-
    ful.

4 Wise men's heart, is within a house of mourning;
and thoughtless people's heart, within a house of
    festivity.

5 There is good to one, for heeding a wise man's
    reproof:
but not to one, though a notable, hearing giddy
    men's singing.

6 Yes, just the cracks of thorns under the kettle;

of such kind is the laughter of the hard-hearted man:

indeed this is a proud breath.

7 But the oppressiveness will make a wise man waver:

as a bribe will corrupt at heart.

8 Morally good! is the result of a cause, rather than its original:

virtuous is a long-winded man, rather than a high-spirited.

9 Do not hurry on in thine equanimity to be vexed:

seeing that provocation useth to settle down

in the bosom of high-stomached ones.

10 Do not say, "how was it? even so that those "former days

"were rich ones, in comparison to these":

for verily! not out of resignation to the Divine will,

enquiredst thou hereupon.

11 Well-being is wisdom, present to a landed possession:

it is even emolument, to the viewers of the Solar rays.

12 Accordingly, persons who are in the shadow of the
     wisdom,

    are in the shadow of the silver:

    still an overpowering quality of knowing is,—

    that a certain science shall preserve in life her
     owners.

13   Learn, with reference to the action of the Deity:

    thinkest thou. that anyone shall be so enabled as
     to amend

    that identical thing, which He hath corrupted?

14 In a day of fertility, be in comfortableness;

    and in a day of unfruitfulness, examine:

    yea this the correlative of that, the Deity hath
     established,

    upon the ground that different to it,

    the earthly man shall find absolutely nothing.

15   To this whole 1 looked,

    in the days of my speculative breath:

    present is a just man, who perisheth in his justness;

    and at hand is an unrighteous one,

    who outstretcheth his days, in injustice.

16 Do not be just, exceedingly;
and thou wilt not outact the very discreet man:
for what? shalt thou destroy thyself.

17 Do not enormously make wilful mistakes,
and do not be an incorrigible:
why shalt thou die! at thine inopportune time.

18 The right is—when thou wilt lay fast hold in this;
when still from that thou wilt not put down thy
hand:
though a fearer of godlike beings,
will go out with each of these dehortations.

19 This wisdom will exert power for the wise man,
to a greater degree than ten having sway,
as have been those identical ones in the city.

20 Because of mere man, none is honest in the land;
to the credit of whom, one sayeth that
he was wont to do the right,
and continued not to miss his step repeatedly.

21 But rather to all the affairs which certain may
litigate,
do not bend thy heart;
in order, that thou may not listen to thy servant,
who actually uttered thine execration.

22 It is past all dispute! yea many times thy heart
    knew;
  how that likewise thyself in particular,
  had spoken evil of other ones!

23   All such, I have put to proof by that wisdom:
  I declared I would get insight;
  but it alas! is remote from me.
24 Distant is that which was;
  ay deep it is! deep; can anyone explain it?

25   I myself with my heart conjoined, have made
    a tour;—
  on purpose to mark and to search;
  and that too striving after wisdom and reckoning:
  to know therefore the injustice induced by obstinacy;
  and the fooleries brought about through foolishness.
26 And I am finding bitterness above death!
  on the side of the woman,—whose self is means of
    catching
  and especially nets whose heart,—bands her hands:
  a man, virtuous in a way pleasing to the Deity,
  shall get away from her;
  but he who doth stray from the right way,
  will be laid hold of by her.

27 Look! I have come upon this,
    Kohéleth himself in pitifulness said:
    "one count relative to another, for getting a reckon-
        ing."

28 It is what repeatedly my soul hath endeavoured,
    and I have not acquired:
    with relation to mankind,
    one man in a count of a thousand I have made
        known;
    though woman in the whole of these, I have not
        discovered.

29 Separately, take a look at this I have found,
    how the Deity hath made this common man artless:
    and yet the same persons possess many sinister
        devisings.

CHAPTER VIII.

1　　　Who ? as much as possible is the sage,
like anyone who actually knoweth the meaning of
　　speech :
wisdom of a human being shall enlighten his face;
then his uncomely aspect will be changed.

2　I am obligated for the keeping of a king's mouth ;
above even an oath, taken by godlike beings.

3　Do not be cast down because of his countenance,
nor go along out of his presence ;
do not, in an iniquitous affair, stand up :
because that anything that he may set his mind upon,
he will effectuate.

4　Inasmuch as a king's word is with power,
is surely anybody habituated to say to him, "how
　　wilt thou ?"

5　Anyone actually keeping a commandment,
will not be acquainted with an evil affair :
and a time carrying judgment
the heart of a discreet man will care for.

6   When for each sort of reigning inclination,
    there is actual existence of a time appending
        judgment:
    is it not? that the detriment of the human being,
    is especially against himself.

7   Because there's not existence of one foreseeing
    what there is that may fall out:
    as a consequence, in pursuance of what it shall arise,
    is there anyone? who will relate about it.

8   Non-existent is mere man, who so domineereth over
    the Wind, that he may shut in against the very
        Wind;
    and non-existent is domination, at the day of death;
    dismission even continueth not in use, in this war:
    therefore wickedness shall not let those escape
    who are possessors of it.

9   At all this I looked—verily making use of my
        heart,
    as respects every sort of conduct, which was acted,
    beneath the resplendent Sun:
    even at a time, when that plebeian man (vile as
        he was)!
    did bear rule over the plebeian man,
    in a way detrimental to himself.

10 Yes in the manner of such kind,—
I did behold wicked men buried, who had come in,
and specially who from a place of the Holy One,
were accustomed to go majestically along;
but who shall be forgotten in that city,
where in so peculiar a way they had acted:
this really, is mere pomposity.

11   Whene'er there is non-existence of sentence being
            executed,
with relation to the injurious deed, quickly;
upon this basis full the heart of the sons of the
            earthly man
is become within them, on purpose to perpetrate sin.

12 When an errant man is in a hundred ways
actually performing wickedness,
and yet is remaining long at it;
then it is that I also am perceiving
how there shall be good to the fearers of the Deity,
who will fear apart from being in His presence.

13 But good shall not be to the lawless man,
and days he shall not make long, after the shadow;
forasmuch as not is he a fearer
apart from being at the faces of godlike beings.

14   There is present murmuring breath,

in the manner that it hath been spent upon the land;

when that there subsist righteous-ones,

where it is causing to come unto them,

like the bad action of the godless-ones;

and that there subsist godless-ones,

where it is causing to reach unto them,

as much as possible the good action of the
righteous-ones.

15   Therefore I myself have praised aloud merriment;

for there is not a good in existence for the plebeian
man,

beneath the resplendent Sun;

but yes! surely to eat and to drink, and so to be
joyous:

and that will join itself to him by his operose habit,

the days of his life! which the Deity gave to him,

under the solar Light.

16   In as far as I adhibited my heart,

to the knowing of experience;

and to inspecting, on the side of the course of life,

which hath been kept upon the land:

for alike in the day, as in the night,—

sleep, in his eyes, there subsisteth not he that seeth.

17 So proportionably I with humility! inspected,
amid the whole of the stirring action of the Deity:
that the earthly man shall not be made capable,
for the discovering of the stirring action, this same,
which hath been established beneath the luminous
   Sun ;
in relation whereto, although the earthly man will
   toil !
on purpose to search out, yet he can not discover:
besides if the scientific man shall declare about
   knowing,
he shall not be made competent for explaining.

CHAPTER IX.

1   But the whole of this here! I did consign
unto my heart,

and so to pick out at all such;

that the just-ones and the skilful, also their depen-
dants,

are within the hand of the Deity:

whether as respects love or hatred!

there is none in existence that knoweth;

it is altogether, at the faces of them.

2   The whole! is extremely that which belongeth to
every one,

a sole blind fortune serving for the just-one and
for the godless,

for the goodly man—or as to the clean or as to
the polluted;

as well for him that actually sacrificeth,

as for him in whose behalf there is non-existent
a sacrificer:

the pious man like the sinful, the sinful like the
pious;

as to the man being sworn trifling! he hath
measure for measure with him, who doth fear an
oath.

3 There is this, which is a detrimental habitude,
in whatsoever was acted, beneath the solar Light;
that one and the same hap-hazard serveth for the
whole:
whereas also the heart of the sons of the human-
kind,
is so filled with wrongful propension,
that infatuation is with their heart, in their lives;
and indeed following it, even unto the corses.

4 As oft as there is anybody, who shall be deservedly
chosen,
towards all the living, there is existing the highest
confidence:
forasmuch as a lively dog, is physically good,—
in comparison to the rending lion, which is a dying
one.

5 So as for the living! knowers they are that they
must die:
but as for the corses, there exist not any of them
cognizant of anything at all!
and there is inexistence further to them, of a hire;
since the mention of them, hath been forsaken.

6 Ev'n their loving—their feeling of hatred too!
   yea their grudging was long ago severed :
   therefore a share is inexistent to them unchangeably,
       for ever ;—
   in anything which hath been made beneath the
       solar Light.

7   Live thou a way of life eating in gladness thy
           bread ;
   and especially drink in heart-ease thy wine :
   forasmuch as a great time
   the Deity hath borne good-will towards thy actions.

8 For any one time, may thy clothes ! be light:
   redolent oil withal, for the sake of thy head do not
       be without.

9 Consort life, with a woman whom thou hast loved :
   every one of the days in the duration of thy
       transitory life,
   which one imparted in thy favour, under the solar
       Light ;
   all while, bounding thy speedily vanishing days ;
   for that same is thine own part, among those alive ;
   even on account of thy labouring ;
   considering that thou thyself art one,

constituted for labour's act, beneath the splendent
    Sun.

10 Each, and every thing! that thou shalt find under
    thy hand,

for effectuating according to thy capacity! perform
    thou:

because there are existent neither making and con-
    triving,

nor science and conception,

is an insatiable underground domain!

whereunto thy very self, is near bearing away.

11   I returned,—to see anon under the solar Light,

that not to the light men tendeth the race,

and not to the strong men the battle;

also that not for the skilled-ones, serveth bread,

and even so not for the discreet-ones, riches;

even also! that not to the understanding-ones,
    supernal favour:

why time purporting a casuality,

is colliding constantly with the whole of them!

12 I protest, that really the common man,

will not mark against his time, equable to the fishes,

the same which are momently being taken by a
    fatal net;

or else in a state of equality with the birds-of-passage ;
just those caught in a certain trap :
e'er as they themselves! mortals snared are the
    sons of the mere man,
when there is a time of harm ;
as soon as it may covertly tumble upon them in a
    moment.

13   However to this degree ! saw I wisdom, under the
    solar Light :
and indeed important it was, for me.

14   An immartial city ;
unarmed men thereat I trow a small number :
that in the direction of her there came a king
    influential,
and round about her he laid siege ;
and indeed set up over her, certain high siege-works.

15   That then one made known in her, an astute
    reduced notable ;
and this personage did let the very city escape,
in the manner of his own expertness :
but as for man in general, he kept not in mind
him, the said impoverished eminent man.

16 Well methought, expertness rather than strength,
   is welfare :

   albeit the skill of this reduced one, is a motor des-
   pised ;

   since his counsels are no more being regarded.

17 Experienced men's words, are in quiet those being
   heard :

   in comparison to the bawling of him,

   that actually governeth over the indocile-ones.

18 Beneficent is knowledge above instruments of conflict:

   whereas a chief sinful one,—

   will destroy well-being amain.

CHAPTER X.

1   Some dead flies shall severally cause to have
      fœtor—
   shall make burst out bubbles, oil of a preparer of
      unguent :
   him, who is estimable from ethic proficiency—from
      gloriousness,
   shall on that wise a little quantity of foolery.

2   An intelligent man's heart maketh for his right
      side ;
   but the ignorant's heart coucheth at his left.

3   And on the road withal, through which the noddy
      is a passer,
   his heart is a senseless one :
   for he observed of the whole, "a lout that one!"

4   If the huffing of the governour mounts up over
      thee,
   thy settledness do thou not cause to fall :
   lo a lenitive will lull to rest big faults.

5 Inherent is evil in what I have seen under the
solar Light:
consimilar with it is inadvertance yea, even going
forth
from before the face of the ruler.

6 The vulgar are inducted into high postures enow:
so rich men shall in the low one dwell.

7 I have beheld slaves upon horses:
chiefs also, I have seen with the eyes
living as much as possible slaves on the land.

8 Who ignoble doth actually dig a pitfall,
he shall fall down therein:
or who breaketh down a fence, him a serpent shall
bite.

9 He nescious who causeth to move stones,
will become affected with pain by their means:
or who cleaveth billets of wood,
will run a hazard with them.

10 If one hath blunted the iron!
and that hewer hath not a forepart edged;
then with valiant arms he will stiffly thump:
howbeit a predominance of making prosper, is
prudence.

11   If the serpent will have bitten, in by no means in-
        cantation :
       behoof existeth not to the owner of lingual sorcery.

12   Oracles of a sage's mouth are divine favour :
       whereas the lips of a coxcomb shall ravenously
        swallow him.

13   The onset of his oral matters, is nonsense :
       and as to the latter stage of his mouth,
       it is a bad, unintelligible jargon.

14   Then as for the predictor, he will bring up matters :
       this ignoble man can not foresee, whatever shall be ;
       and that which shall arise late in time following
        him,
       is there anyone who can foreshow to him ?

15   The bodily labour of the fatigable wretches,
       shall harass each of them piteously :
       so that he shall have not known, as respects going
        to town.

16   Woe to thee, O Land ! whose king is a boy :
       as thy chiefs into the dawn will eat.

17   Oh ! the felicities of thy noble self, Land,—
       whose king is a son of Horite rulers :
       thy chiefs, therefore, at a natural time will eat ;
       in prowess, and by no means in character of drink-
        ing.

18 In a two-fold sloth, this raftering will part itself
  asunder:

  then in a hanging down of both hands, this house
  will drip.

19 Up to laughter, some are entertaining an eating;

  for as to wine, it shall cause life to joy in jollity:

  and indeed the silver shall answer with the whole.

20 Even then in thy conception,

  one who is a regal personage do not thou execrate:

  and in rooms—no not in that one of the lying
  down of thyself,

  do thou execrate a rich personage:

  for the volant creature of the sky, will carry the
  veritable voice;

  and the possessor of the pair of wings will blaze a
  report.

CHAPTER XI.

1   It suiteth to send thy bread-seed over the watery surface:
because that at enough of the days thou shalt obtain several.

2 Deal out a dole unto seven, so too unto eight:
even notwithstanding that thou canst not foresee,
in what way distress may arise upon this land.

3 As oft as the lowery skies shall be filled with sweepy rain,
over the territory they will pour out;
so then certainly may fall timber! in the South;
or unquestionably in the North;
as for place! where this timber may have fallen,
there that will have arisen.

4   A presager who actually mindeth wind, will not scatter seed:
so an augur gazing up in disquiet on the lowers,
will not harvest.

5 As there is inexistence of thine own self compre-
hending

what is the course of action of the Divine Spirit;

at the time of osseous compacture,

within the belly of the female going with young:

in a high degree so! thou canst not understand,

concerning the efficience of the Deity;

which useth to effectuate at the whole.

6 In the opening of day, strew with thy seed;

but before the even do thou not give rest to thy
hand:

seeing that thou subsistest not one prescient,

where? may this sprout, one or another; and where

may indubitably both of them, alike as to sort, be
good together.

7 Both in sweetness is early light,

and it is pleasure for the eyes, to view with the
Solar rays.

8 Then if years many a time over! the plebeian man
will survive,

in the whole of them he shall be joyous:

he also shall call to mind, as to the days of the
darkness;

forasmuch as immoderate they shall be,

every one which arriveth being rueful breath!

9 Joyous be thou, fine youth! along thy childhood:
belike thy heart will make thee good-humoured,
along the days of thy youthhood:
as well proceed thou fast! in the tracks of thy
    heart,
as in the scenes, entrancing thine eyes:
but early experience thou, that spite of all these,
the Deity will cause thee to come in for the judg-
    ment.

10 Howbeit turn away chagrin out of thy heart,
and make thou vice pass over, off thy flesh:
without doubt the childhood and the hopeful
    dawning,
are breath wanting judgment.

CHAPTER XII.

1   Thereupon be mindful of thy creators;
along the days of thy youthhood :
as long as that the days of declining shall not
    come in,
and that years shall have not made touch ;
concerning which thou shalt observe—
" there is to me in them no existence of gratifi-
    cation !"

2 The while that the beamy Sun and the lamp,
or the changing moon and the orbed stars,
shall not be obscured :
and that the lowers shall not return,
on the back part of the pelting shower.

3 In the character of that day ! when *the arms*,
those Guarders of the building will shake :
and when *the legs*, those frail Men of prowess,
will have bent themselves :
and indeed when *the teeth*,
those tiny Grinding-implements, will have left off,
since they were ofttimes diminished ;

and when *the eyes,* those diminutive Lookers,

inside the latticed light-holes, will have become blindish.

4   When withal *the mandibles,*

this bi-valve Door toward the avenue, will have been shut up,

in that there is a sinking, as to the din of manducation:

during which *the ear* will start up! even to the note of the bird;

and all *the articulate voices,* those Daughters of singing,

will extraordinarily be brought low.

5   Also when some for any thing of height will fear,

as utterly terrified ones in the journey;

when both the Almond-tree will shed its blossoms,

and the springy Grasshopper will be burthensome;

when ev'n, as to a particular natural impulse,

it will come to naught:

verily the mortal is setting forward,

unto the dwelling-place of his perpetualness;

ay those audible ones who are lamenting,

have encompassed round about at the street.

6 Awhile that this little silvery chain,

the *Spinal Bones*, shall not be unlinked :

nor this golden oil-vase, *the Skull*, be broken in :

and that this earthern jar, *the Ribbed Breast*,

shall not be broken in pieces, over this fountain,

the *Heart ;*

nor this rundlet, *the Belly*,

be dinged against this pit, *the Pelvis*.

7 Thus shall moulder this earth, *the Carcase!* over

the land,

as much as possible that which it had been :

whereas this wind, *the Vital Spirit*,

shall return to that Deity, which had emitted her.

8 Wasted thing of wasted things! said a person,

Kohéleth ;

the whole is a counterfeit entity !

9 Well as for what is over and above ;

it is that Kohéleth was a Rabbi :

uninterruptedly, instilled he principles into the

people ;

he also discriminatingly and very searchingly

adjusted proverbial sentences to a great degree.

10   Kohéleth sought studiously, in order to find,
      matters of delight severally at least written rightly,
      an instance, precepts of trustiness.

11   Precepts of masters, how truly they are ox-goads !
      so truly also are they guards fixed,
      as for proprietors of collections of ·sheep :
      brought forth they were, from The Only One
           Shepherd.

12   I do enjoin moreover ;—
      from amongst them receive thou, my son ! a help :
      to the composing of writings by adequate ideas,
      there not inheres a final one ;
      while protractive reading, is expenditure of flesh.

13   At a closing of speech, there is the whole being
           listened to :
      of the Godhead be thou afraid !
      and specially to his commandments attend strictly ;
      lo this is the whole grace of every man's calling.

14   The deduction is, that every deed
      He—the Godhead !—will bring in into judgment,
      in spite of all at present shrouded :
      if ethically it is good, else if it is sinful.

THE END.

www.ingramcontent.com/pod-product-compliance
Lightning Source LLC
Chambersburg PA
CBHW021528090426
42739CB00007B/841